Exploring HURT With Your Child

Written by Ilene L. Dillon, M.S.W.

Exploring HURT With Your Child

Written by Ilene L. Dillon, M.S.W.

Enchanté Publishing, Palo Alto, California, U.S.A.

Enchanté Publishing
120 Hawthorne
Palo Alto, CA 94301
1 (800) 473-2363

ISBN 1-56844-070-7

Series concept by Ayman Sawaf and Gudrun Höy
Series format, art direction, and design by Romney Lange
Edited by Gudrun Höy, Lynne Piade, and Linda Hull

Printed in the United States of America

First Edition

10 9 8 7 6 5 4 3 2 1

It was with great pleasure that I accepted Enchanté's invitation to participate in its Emotional Literacy™ campaign. For nearly 30 years I have worked intimately with hundreds of people who suffered daily from being "at the mercy of," rather than "in charge of," their emotions. Emotions can be directed, used as guideposts, and can enhance daily life.

Enchanté offers a unique companion series exploring the emotions—jealousy, anger, guilt, grief, loneliness, fear, and hurt—which help parents, children, and educators develop Emotional Literacy™ in their lives. Children can read the picture book *William's Gift*, process hurt feelings through the activity book *Exploring Hurt*, and engage in creative activities in partnership with their parents in *Exploring Hurt With Your Child*. Each product provides techniques that underscore the importance of imagination and recognizing and releasing emotions constructively while building self-esteem.

I have found few resources which offer as thorough and understandable a framework for working with the emotions as the Lazaris materials published by Concept Synergy in Florida. In addition, I have been influenced by the inspiring work of Marcus Books in Toronto, Canada, and the works of family therapy pioneer Virginia Satir; Menninger Foundation psychotherapist Harriet Goldhor Lerner, Ph.D.; the excellent offerings of Jim Fay and Foster Cline of Colorado's Cline-Fay Institute; and books by Adele Faber and Elaine Mazlish. These sources along with my years of clinical and teaching experience, have shaped the psychological theories presented in this series.

I am grateful for the opportunity to share my experience with others for the benefit of today's children, who will need to stay balanced and in charge of themselves in a fast-paced and challenging world.

Millions of parents have said "I'm teaching my child this so s/he won't have to go through the pain I have gone through." We parents do a lot to assure ourselves that our beloved children do not feel hurt. Hurt is painful. We can protect our children from most physical hurt. Protection from emotional hurt is more difficult. Sometimes we, unwittingly, cause the hurt. Sometimes hurt cannot be avoided.

Like any emotion, however, hurt offers us an opportunity to learn. A real emotion, hurt has both negative and positive aspects. Negatively, hurt causes pain and discomfort, destroys feelings of love, and shreds our self-image, self-esteem, and self-confidence. Positively, hurt shows us where we are "thinking small," where we are allowing ourselves to be victimized, and where we are not utilizing our personal power. Hurt can teach us the importance of setting firm personal limits.

While it is not necessary to experience hurt in order to create positive change, most people don't risk change until their pain increases to the point where they feel they have no other choice. Even though it is difficult to watch, most of the hurt your child encounters is important for him/her to experience, so that s/he will feel impetus to grow and change. It is important that parents do not try to smooth things over quickly in an attempt to distract their child from the hurtful experience. We must teach our children how to recognize and use their emotional hurt as a basis for learning, so that they do not have to repeat hurtful experiences.

The suggestions and activities in this booklet are in no way intended as a substitute for professional psychotherapy. If you determine that the feelings of hurt expressed by your child are more intense than you can handle, get help for yourself and your child from a professional therapist, a caring and non-judgmental relative, a member of the clergy, or a friend. Anyone with a history of mental disorder should not attempt these activities without first consulting a qualified mental health professional.

Our emotional energy takes the form of hurt when: *a)* our picture of how the world operates is challenged, and *b)* the outside world seems to fail to recognize "who we really are." For example, your young child may have the belief that it is your job, as parent, to be available every time s/he needs you. If you are not available, your child will experience feelings of anger, and under the anger, hurt. The idea that your child has held of how his/her world operates has been challenged.

In our society, emotion has taken a backseat to intellect. People have learned to explain "why" they feel a certain way, and often feel ashamed if they don't have a good reason to explain their emotions. We feel at a disadvantage for having emotions. Nowhere is this more true than with feelings of hurt. A man who acknowledges hurt is judged harshly and negatively. A woman is expected to express hurt feelings, yet this is perceived as part of what makes her the "weaker sex." We all experience hurt; and both sexes pay a high price for acknowledging that hurt. We learn very early to avoid admitting to hurt feelings when we really feel them. Simultaneously, it has become acceptable to use "hurt feelings" as a tool to manipulate others by admitting to hurt we really do not feel. Children of a very young age learn this, making it difficult, indeed, to tell which hurts that people report are "real" and which are "not real."

For example, many young children will accost their parents: "You hurt my feelings when you made me go to bed!" Or, "You hurt my feelings when you said you were tired and didn't want to play with me." Parents, intent upon being good and loving to their children, struggle to understand such statements without drowning in a sea of guilt. Does our child really feel hurt? Is it not all right to say we feel tired? Or, is our child astutely reading that we respond immediately to someone saying "You hurt me," and thus experimenting with what kind of control s/he can have over us by using this ploy unconsciously? If this behavior goes unchecked, a child will continue to manipulate with hurt, causing untold damage in the family and to him/herself.

The Damage Hurt Creates

Emotional hurt destroys feelings of love. Just as feelings of love dissipate in a marriage when the two partners do one thing after another that is hurtful to each other, so repeated emotional hurt between parents and children destroys the love between them. Parents who perceive their children's actions as "designed to hurt" will feel less love for them. Children who feel unloved will have a hard time developing into loving adults. When it is possible to rebuild bonds of love, it can take a long, long time.

Emotional hurt also damages the way a child relates to him/herself. Hurt shreds a child's self-image (the idea each child has of who s/he really is). Hurt stimulates anger that is held inside so the hurt is not exposed. The held-in anger tears apart the self-esteem (the value your child places upon him/herself and his/her actions, experiences and accomplishments). The feeling of being "victimized" instead of empowered undermines a child's self-confidence (the ability your child has to rely upon him/herself).

Parents are not able to keep the world from presenting their child with hurtful experiences. Nor can they keep themselves from ever hurting their child's feelings. Simply due to the fact that your child has a different personality, personal rhythm, and temperament than you, the way you act will hurt your child's feelings at one time or another. However, parents can help their children avoid the potential, tremendously negative impact of hurt by teaching them how to recognize, process, and release hurt. The ideas and activities offered in this booklet, and its companion books *William's Gift* and *Exploring Hurt*, have been designed to assist you in this task.

Hurt takes time to heal, unlike anger, which surfaces and passes through us quickly. Hurt surfaces and then makes its way out slowly, festering and shredding aspects of the self while it passes through. Our emotional self takes a lot of time to rebuild, one layer at a time, like the body does in healing a serious burn. Hurt compounds when parents do not believe, respect, or deal effectively with real hurt that their child is experiencing. When hurt feelings "pile up," layer upon layer of "emotional scar tissue" builds up and can be very difficult to heal.

After the same hurtful experience is repeated several times, a child will develop a belief system that supports that hurtful experience. Unless corrected, your child will unconsciously use this belief as a "self-fulfilling prophecy." For example, when a child has felt hurt many times by a parent, s/he can develop a belief which says "People I love hurt me," and watch every loving relationship s/he has for signs of potential or actual hurt. Your child will soon find him/herself creating the hurt in which s/he believes, becoming the brunt of an increasing number of hurtful experiences. If this internal belief is not changed before your child reaches adulthood, s/he will look back in life and offer indisputable "proof" supporting that belief. In short, your child will have developed into a person whose primary role in life is "victim."

You and your child can avoid this devastating way of relating to the world by working consciously and effectively with hurt feelings. As a parent, you are instrumental in setting the tone for your child's life. You can take care to eliminate as many hurtful actions and statements from your vocabulary as possible, examine and rectify hurt feelings that your child reports to you, and assist your child in acknowledging, processing, and healing hurts as s/he encounters them.

Hurt as a Manipulative Tool

A big challenge to dealing effectively with hurt is people's use of hurt as a manipulative tool. Because acknowledging real hurt is discouraged by society and a majority of children and adults are rewarded for manipulative (rather than direct or assertive) behavior, many people routinely attempt to control the behavior of others by reporting or threatening emotional hurt. Distinguishing between real hurt and manipulative hurt is difficult, and something you may not be able to do even with your very young child.

People use hurt to manipulate others either passively (defensively) or aggressively (offensively). For example, "You better not take my pancakes away, or else it will hurt my feelings," says your three-year-old (defensively), with downcast eyes and chin tucked to chest. "If you don't turn on the TV right now, I will stop being your friend!" (aggressively) promises your four- or five-year-old. As these typical statements by children illustrate, a child attempts to control the behavior of a parent through the use of hurt.

Parents manipulate with hurt, too. "You don't care about me or my feelings when you refuse to write my parents a thank-you letter! I hope you never hurt me that way again!" a parent says (offensively) to a thirteen-year-old. "It's okay. You do what you think is best. I'll be fine without you," says a parent whose tone is more revealing of hurt (passively) than even the words. "Don't you know how you hurt me when you get angry with me?" whines a parent who has learned to play "victim" (passive). "Please don't say anything to your mother," pleads a father, "or she might get hurt." Now the whole family is being passively manipulated to behave in a particular way to avoid the effects of threatened hurt feelings.

Most of us can look at our everyday lives, sadly, and find numerous examples of people manipulating either passively or aggressively with emotional hurt. When we have this awareness, yet allow the behavior, we are knowingly allowing others to hurt us, destroying love and shredding vital aspects of ourselves. Parents can help their children recognize hurt that is used to manipulate, and empower them to block that behavior.

Identifying Manipulation

The way to tell whether the hurt being expressed is real or a manipulation attempt is by paying attention to our other feelings. Since society routinely encourages people to ignore, repress, or suppress all but the "positive" feelings (an impossible task!), most of us do not use our feelings the way they were designed, as signals which can guide us through our everyday lives. When this conditioning is overcome, and each of us listens to and lives by our feelings, life's path is easier to negotiate. This is especially true in identifying manipulation.

Feelings that signal manipulation include:

- ☛ Anger (usually felt stronger than the situation really merits);
- ☛ Guilt (a form of anger turned inward);
- ☛ Confusion
- ☛ Exhaustion

Other warning signals include: a knot or uncomfortable feeling in the stomach; strong feeling of wanting to escape; and/or a neutral or unfeeling response to tears or other strong release of feelings by another person.

These telltale feelings or "gut" responses will occur immediately as you relate to others who might be trying to manipulate you. Especially when several warning feelings occur together, you can safely draw the conclusion that you are being manipulated. Once you know that you are being manipulated, you or your child will need to decide whether or not to allow the manipulation to continue.

Four Good Techniques to Block Manipulation

❶ BREAK CONTACT

Turn your back, leave the room or area, or hang up the telephone. Especially with young children, this break in contact does not have to be long (30 seconds is sufficient, and powerful, too). Longer breaks can be hurtful!

❷ EXPOSE THE MANIPULATION

Make a statement about your feelings. For example, "Since you said what you did to me, I notice a tightness in my solar plexus (tummy). That usually means I am being manipulated. Is there something you want from me that you are not saying?" (To openly state that you are being manipulated by another person merely brings a vigorous protest or counter-attack. Be sure to speak only in terms of your own feelings to avoid this reaction.)

❸ SET GOALS FOR YOURSELF AND STICK TO THEM, "BROKEN RECORD" STYLE

"I know you are angry with me for my decision, and (not 'but') my answer to your request is still 'no.'"

❹ DEVELOP AND STICK TO AN AUTOMATIC PROCEDURE FOR SPECIFIC, REPEATED BEHAVIORS

"Do you know what I do when my child whines instead of using words to ask for something? I go away for a few minutes and come back later."

Be prepared for a strong reaction when you block your child's attempt to manipulate with hurt. In fact, your child may try out every manipulative behavior s/he knows that has worked for him/her in the past! Use care not to fall prey to this behavior. If you give in to the manipulations even once, you will have to start all over again in blocking manipulative behavior. Similar to when your child was two years old and having temper tantrums, remove yourself and maintain a comfortable distance, staying as emotionally neutral as you can, allowing the tantrum-like behavior to run its course. Then, empathize but don't sympathize: allow for hurt feelings while remembering your child's need to resolve the hurt in ways that are right for him/herself. Your child will eventually be grateful to you for not giving in to his/her manipulation, though on the surface s/he will push for you to do so.

After you successfully hold off your child's attempts to manipulate by using hurt, explain to your child what you did and why. For example, "I have decided that I'm not going to let people hurt me to get me to do what they want. When you said "———" to me, it hurt me; so I decided not to let you behave that way with me. I went away for a few minutes and came back, so you could try another way of talking to me." By doing this, you will be teaching your child through both actions and words not to allow others to manipulate him/her using the threat or promise of hurt. You will be teaching your child personal empowerment, helping him/her to preserve feelings of love, and safeguarding his/her self-image, self-esteem, and self-confidence.

Some families pass down patterns of "victim" or "victimizer," (characteristic of people who manipulate with hurt or the threat of hurt), from one generation to another. A parent who plays the role of "victim," for example, tends to parent children who intimidate. As they become intimidating parents, their offspring in turn become victims. You can help your child end generations-long negative patterns by blocking manipulative behaviors that employ hurt when they first appear.

Recognizing a Hurt Child

Carrying around hurt over time, as with any strong emotion, will tend to multiply its negative aspects and inhibit your child from experiencing a full life. Look for your child to "curl up" physically when hurt, hanging his/her head, holding his/her stomach, wailing, gazing at the floor, and becoming teary-eyed.

A CHILD WHO HAS EXPERIENCED REPEATED HURT MAY EXHIBIT THESE CHARACTERISTICS:

- ☛ Withdrawal
- ☛ Irritability
- ☛ Callousness
- ☛ Lowered self-esteem
- ☛ Anger
- ☛ Non-assertiveness
- ☛ Loneliness
- ☛ Aloofness or superior attitude
- ☛ Vigilance, in anticipation of getting hurt
- ☛ Deliberately hurtful to others
- ☛ Lowered ability to trust self and others

As children grow up and gain life experience, they will feel and experiment with most, if not all, of these behaviors. If your child displays these reactions and behaviors a few times, there is no cause for concern. However, if your child has experienced repeated hurt or exhibits several of these characteristics together over a prolonged period of time, s/he may have a problem dealing with hurt. The repercussions of holding onto hurt are not life-threatening. Holding onto hurt can, however, reduce the effectiveness and overall quality of your child's life if it is not addressed and replaced with empowerment.

If your child demonstrates an inability to process or release feelings of hurt, consider these three questions: ***a)*** Is your child repeatedly being hurt emotionally by someone close to him/her?; ***b)*** Does your child have a personality for which change or "letting go" is difficult?; and ***c)*** Are you (or another adult close to your child) holding onto hurt, experiencing repeated hurts, or acting as a lifelong "victim?" If any of these is true, use your observation to face the fact that hurt is a problem in your family, and work on it in the ways set out in this booklet. In addition, get therapeutic help. A knowledgeable professional can assist you with feelings of hurt (which may seem overwhelming to you to work on alone), and help you and your child make swift, effective, and lasting changes in these strong patterns.

What do children need from adults when they have emotional reactions?

 **Validation:** "You have feelings and it is okay and understandable that you have them;"

 **Empathy:** "I can see that upsets you," or "Most people feel angry when that happens;"

 **Room to feel:** "Let me hold you while you cry," or "Maybe you need a few minutes to be upset before we talk;"

 **Talk:** "Please tell me what hurt your feelings," or "Let's talk about situations like that and how they happen;"

 **Opportunity to learn:** There is a lesson in each experience and an opportunity to develop a plan for next time. Children need guidance in this, but please remember not to push help if it is not wanted. Wait until your child asks for it, or gives a very clear "yes" when you offer help.

Facing the Fact of Emotional Hurt

The most effective thing you can do is to make hurt a legitimate feeling in your family. When real hurt is validated, imagined or made-up hurt will not be used as a manipulative tool. You and your child can work together to feel, process, and release the emotional energy of hurt, using its occurrence as a catalyst for seeking ways to gain personal empowerment. Help your child conquer hurt feelings by teaching him/her how to face the hurt and move it through him/her. Just the act of looking squarely at what has actually happened and what has actually been hurtful ("facing the fact") frees your child from some of the pain. Show your child how to handle hurt instead of protecting him/her from life experiences or rescuing him/her by making things "all better!"

Each person is capable of directing his/her own emotional release. With long-repressed, intensified feelings, however, it is still best to use the guidance and support of a person with greater knowledge and experience, such as a therapist, counselor, social worker, or member of the clergy. Even though releasing feelings is a natural activity and not to be feared, long-repressed feelings tend to grow in power. They can be frightening and painful as they find their way out of us. But children, especially younger ones, whose emotional patterns are less entrenched, release feelings easily. Your help will be enough to heal many hurts, as well as to teach your child the process for healing hurt on his/her own.

While processing emotions, people feel very vulnerable. To facilitate facing and processing feelings of hurt, provide a safe, and supportive atmosphere for working with feelings. If a child shares his/her feelings a few times and feels endangered by doing so, s/he will close down again. So that you and your child can have successful healing experiences, respect your child's confidences.

Guidelines and Helpful Hints

1. Create a time and a place to work with feelings.

2. As much as possible, allow your child to be totally truthful about his/her feelings. Be willing to accept that your words or actions may have been felt as "hurt" by your child. Even if you are seen as the "cause," allow your child to share his/her hurt without judgment, defensiveness, unsolicited advice, or retribution. As your child states or processes feelings, remind yourself: "That is my child over there in that body saying s/he has been hurt (and s/he is the person who needs to learn to deal with hurt). This is me in this body feeling bad (guilty) or sad regarding him/her."

3. Resolve to protect your child from backlash due to statements made during emotional processing time. Except in extreme displays of emotion, make a pact with yourself to think things over for a few days (without talking with others about it, so you can have the full power of your own reactions) before you take action or seek help.

4. Give value to all thoughts and feelings. You may feel your child is "making mountains out of molehills." Recognize that experiences are a lot more emotionally intense for children than for adults, who have learned through years of experience. Although it may not always be easy to tell whether a hurt expressed by your child is real or an attempt to manipulate, err on the side of "real."

5. You and your child do not have to agree on how you see the world. Be grateful for the fact that you and your child are sharing your deepest thoughts and feelings and partnering each other for growth.

6. If you offer help and get anything other than a clear "yes," don't insist. People are most empowered when they find their own solutions to painful situations.

7. Follow your own feelings and guidance from your child about touching, holding, or comforting.

❽ If the feelings you hear expressed by your child are difficult for you to handle, get help for yourself and your child from a therapist, a caring (and non-judgmental) relative, a member of the clergy, or a friend. These activities are not intended as a substitute for professional psychotherapy. Children need to know that their feelings do not scare or overwhelm the adults around them. To know that you will take care of yourself, disallow abuse or get help for situations that are too difficult for you gives your child the message that, as the adult, you are in charge. Besides benefiting from support for yourself, this is comforting to your child.

❾ Encourage your child to develop creative choices for handling hurt "next time." Learning to search for new, more effective ways of living strengthens your child for independent, adult life. Your child's solution may seem risky or difficult to you. When your child finds an empowering solution, check that s/he feels good about following this path and see whether the solution will create inconvenience or hurt for anyone else. If your child seems determined, and others will not be hurt, allow your child to try out his/her solution. It is easier for your child to learn what does and does not work when s/he is young and can fall back to the comfort of a parent's arms, rather than waiting until adulthood to go through this process.

❿ Remember that each of us is ultimately in charge of how we emotionally experience an event. Therefore, when you share your own feelings of hurt with your child, do not make him/her responsible for your feelings by saying "You hurt my feelings." Instead, take care to say "I felt hurt when you said ———." This way, you are in charge of translating the act to hurt or non-hurt. You also model this behavior for your child.

⓫ Remember that as you do hurt-releasing activities with your child, you are also most likely healing hurt in yourself. Allow time and space to absorb these releases. Keeping seperate journals may prove to be useful to you and your child.

Hurt-Releasing Activities

The activities that follow are divided into three categories:

PREVENTIVE

activities which act to prevent the buildup of hurt feelings;

PROCESSING

activities which release hurt already being carried by your child; and

HEALING

activities which help heal hurt feelings and assist your child in setting limits.

With all activities, if making a mess is a concern, purchase an inexpensive plastic shower curtain, and include laying it out on the floor as part of your ritual in releasing feelings. Complete the activity as soon as your child shows signs of losing interest. *If your child would like his/her friends to participate in any of the activities, make sure to obtain permission from the parents of your child's friends before including them.*

When you participate in these activities with your child, your words and actions convey the message that the different feelings about hurt are normal human feelings which are okay to have and to express. Together you both can work on healing your hurts and learning how not to become a victim of emotional hurt. Enthusiasm, support, and fun in a relaxed atmosphere are strong guarantees of effectiveness. Trust the process of using feelings to further personal growth.

ACTIVITY #1

Name the Feeling

Purpose: To help your child become familiar with emotions and develop the ability to *a)* recognize feelings; *b)* name feelings; *c)* know how to identify particular feelings by feel and sight; and *d)* communicate feelings.

Rationale: Children not in the habit of sharing their true feelings with others are more likely to use hurt manipulatively. Since claiming hurt feelings is not fully respected by society, a child who already has difficulty recognizing, naming, and sharing feelings is handicapped in learning to communicate when s/he feels hurt. This activity teaches your child to become comfortable with recognizing and communicating hurt, as well as with sharing feelings.

Tools: A large piece of paper, and washable marker pens, crayons, or colored pencils.

:s 5–8 Invite your child to play a game about feelings with you. When s/he accepts, begin by naming as many feelings as you can think of together. Make a list of these feelings (lonely, excited, angry, jealous, sad, peaceful, afraid, grateful, safe, happy, guilty, hurt, hopeful, relaxed, joyful, etc.). Go through your list together, talking about how each emotion feels. Take turns acting out the feeling, showing it on your face as well as in your body. When the idea of the feeling is well-established for your child, ask him/her to make an illustration of a person expressing that feeling with the name next to it. Making your list, acting it out, and illustrating it may take you more than one activity period. Be willing to take a break whenever your child shows signs of fatigue. During the break, you may think of more emotions you wish to add to the list.

Once your list has been completed, you can play "Name the Feeling" with your child whenever you want to build your child's ability to work with his/her emotions. Display your chart at your child's eye level. Point to an emotion and its illustration and ask your child to act it out (with body and face). Then say aloud: "I feel ——— (insert name of feeling) right now." Take turns pointing to feelings and acting them out with your child.

After playing this game a few times, you can ask your child to name what s/he is experiencing whenever you notice an emotional reaction. Your child will become increasingly conversant with his/her feelings, and will develop a lifelong ability to identify and share feelings with others.

AGES 9–11 The activity is the same. Your older child may enjoy a deeper exploration of feelings, by playing this game with a group. The members of your group can explore how many different ways a particular feeling can be expressed and whether it looks the same way regardless who exhibits it. Another topic for discussion is how it feels to be around someone who is expressing a particular feeling.

AGES 12–14 The activity is the same. Young teens enjoy drama. They also like to imitate others. You can vary this activity by asking if they know anyone famous, or a television or movie actor who characteristically exhibits certain feelings, imitating them in the way that person expresses the feelings. Your young teen may also enjoy the challenge of seeing how quickly s/he can switch from one feeling to another. Emotions can be dramatized, without naming them ahead of time, allowing an audience (even of one person) to guess which emotion is being demonstrated as in the game of charades.

ACTIVITY #2

Who Is In Charge of My Feelings?

Purpose: To teach your child that s/he has a choice in all experiences, and to offer practice in choosing his/her emotional reactions.

Rationale: People often attribute their feelings to the actions or statements of others. "You hurt my feelings" is a phrase unhappy children use with their parents. Each person has a choice about how another's behavior is accepted and processed. Ultimately, we all have a choice about whether we react to an action with feelings of "hurt" or with another feeling. How we perceive actions affects how we feel about them. This activity helps to prevent hurt feelings by encouraging a change in perception and by showing experientially that other choices of "how to feel" are available.

Tools: Imagination and a sense of fun. Paper and pen for a list.

5–8 Fold an 8½-by-11-inch sheet of paper in half lengthwise, and invite your child to think about the things that someone might do or say that would hurt his/her feelings. Write down those things on the left hand side of the page.

Ask your child if s/he would like to practice saying or acting out those things with you in order to experiment with different ways to react. If your child is not ready for this part of the activity, DO NOT force it; try again later.

If your child is ready, choose one of the items on your list and act it out together. Ask your child to make you the "victim" first by saying the "hurtful thing" to you. React as your child would—crying, accusing him/her of hurting your feelings, etc. This usually brings laughter, sometimes even comfort for your child.

Next, look at the situation from a different perspective. An alternate response to hurtful or angry remarks could be, for example: "I feel hurt by this; and I don't let other people hurt me. I like myself too much. So I will say 'Please talk to me another way. That way does not help me feel good inside.'" Try acting out this alternative and saying it aloud. List each new option on the right hand side of your sheet of paper. Every time you think of another option, acknowledge aloud "I feel hurt," then revisit the scene using the new option. (Repeat this activity one to three times until you are comfortable using it.)

Discuss with your child which option works the best, feels the best, or provides the greatest opportunity for change. Include this idea: Even when our feelings are hurt, we have a choice about whether to stay "hurt and victimized" or whether to process the hurt and empower ourselves to feel good. Talk about and practice either speaking up or getting away from a hurtful situation in order to feel better. End your activity by asking your child to make a commitment to him/herself to "bring in another feeling" the next time s/he feels hurt.

Ages 9–11 The activity is the same. Encourage your child to draw a picture on a piece of folded paper, with the incident and hurt reaction depicted on the left; the desired non-hurt reaction depicted on the right. Older children enjoy doing arts and crafts to finish their learning. Banners made of burlap stitched with yarn that state the intended reaction to hurtful situations are also fun.

Ages 12–14 Be very careful with young teens using this activity. Their feelings are easily hurt. To protect from directly hurting each others' feelings, imagine that other people (friends, famous people, well-liked adults) have the potentially hurtful experiences, and that the solutions worked out are not your child's but theirs. This provides a layer of frequently-needed protection for your teen while still teaching him/her to be in charge of feelings.

ACTIVITY #3

Taking the Sting from Criticism

Purpose: To provide your child with two techniques that can be used to divert criticism and reduce hurt.

Rationale: Children and adults of all ages judge and criticize others. Criticism is often used to hurt people. It especially hurts when the criticism has a grain of truth to it. When a person knows how to separate his/her sense of self-esteem from the criticism of another, hurt can be reduced and/or avoided. Your child will feel a sense of empowerment in knowing how to maintain his/her self-esteem when critical barbs are aimed his/her way. In addition, since most people seek a reaction to their behavior from others, critics will get less attention from your child and either quit their criticizing or move on to someone who gives a bigger reaction (puts out more energy in reaction to criticism!).

Tools: Paper and a pen or pencil for making a list to which you and your child can refer, that names the two "cue words" for turning aside criticism.

5–8 As part of a general discussion about criticism, when your child is not feeling hurt, say, "I learned that there are some things I can say aloud so that when people say mean things to me (criticize), it doesn't hurt as much. Would you like me to teach you what I learned?" Only if your child is receptive to this invitation, proceed.

VALIDATION:

Validating another person's right to have an opinion, without agreeing with that opinion

"Usually when somebody says a mean thing, there is a little truth to it, even though most of it is not true. It's hard to remember right then that even if what that person says *were* true, they don't have to tell us in a mean way. So the first trick when someone talks in a mean way is to say, 'You think that, but it isn't the way I think.' Will you practice it with me so we can see how this works?" When your child agrees, continue by saying, "This is just for practice. I'm going to say a mean thing (criticize) about how you are dressed. When I do that, you say 'You think,' and then say exactly what I said to you."

Adult: *"Your shirt is ugly."* Coach your child to repeat the words: *"You think my shirt is ugly."* Encourage him/her by complimenting the behavior. Make sure to have your child make a statement rather than ask a question.

Adult: *"Yes, why did you pick such a terrible color for today?"*

Child: *"You think I picked a terrible color for today."*

Adult: *"Of course you did. I can see it right there."*

Child: *"You think you can see it right there."*

Continue practicing this technique until you and your child get a clear feeling of what happens to the critical energy. Stop and discuss what you are both feeling. Because the critical energy is being funneled past your child, rather than being taken directly into his/her heart, your child may report having fun, feeling good, or liking the game. Talk about how it feels if you don't say "you think" when someone says a mean thing. As critic, you will feel like you are running out of critical statements. You might feel disappointment in the unexpected reaction of the person you are criticizing. When you complete this brief discussion, change roles and repeat the experience. Again, review feelings. Proceed to the next technique.

ACCEPTANCE:

Accepting the probability of truth within the criticism, without agreeing that it is currently true.

"This time, I'm going to say something that you know is sometimes true for you. But you don't know if it is true right now. For example, I could say 'Your hair is messy.' You know that sometimes your hair is messy and sometimes it is not. Do you know whether it is messy right now?" Your child may respond

"No." Then say to your child, "When you don't know, then use the word 'Sometimes,' and say back what I say to you. This time, you would say 'Sometimes my hair is messy.' Are you ready to try this?" With assent, continue. Start with easy examples.

Adult: *"Your hair is messy."*

Child: *"Sometimes my hair is messy."*

Adult: *"That's because you don't look in a mirror to see if your hair is neat."*

Child: *"Sometimes I don't look in a mirror."*

Adult: *"You don't care if your hair is messy and makes it difficult for you to see."*

Child: *"Sometimes I don't care if my hair is messy."*

As you work with this technique, let your child attempt to respond on his/her own. Limited coaching is okay to keep things moving.

Just as with the validation technique, exchange statements several times and then review how each of you is feeling. Trust that preventive learning is taking place, especially if your child appears to be having a good time. As before, switch places and report feelings after each exchange. Point out to your child that validation and acceptance of criticism do not help people to feel close to each other. They just help take the sting out of the "mean words."

Before ending the activity, criticize each other and intermix the two techniques. If more than one criticism occurs at a time, encourage your child to pick the easiest one (usually the last one mentioned) to include in the technique. These two techniques can be used by all the members of your family. Encourage yourself and your child(ren) to practice them until they become habit. If you forget to use the techniques yourself the next time your child says "You are a mean parent because you won't let me have this treat," when you catch yourself, correct mid-behavior, so your child can see you doing so. "Oh, I forgot. You think I am mean." You could also say "Sometimes

I am a mean parent" or "What is it about my decision that makes you think I am mean?" Even though both you and your child know you are using the techniques, the practice can still be effective!

AGES 9–11 The activity is the same. Children this age can handle criticism better, so your critical statements can be stronger. Give criticisms which may seem a little harsh to you (still using care to observe your child's personal limits and sensitivities). As your child learns to deal effectively with criticism you offer in these artificial practice sessions, his/her ability to deal with criticism encountered in the real world will improve.

AGES 12–14 The activity is the same. Young teens and teenagers, although sensitive to criticism, can be extremely harsh critics, so these techniques can prevent a lot of hurt and emotional pain. If working with the techniques directly is too difficult, watch a video, movie, or television show in which people criticize each other, and use the situations in the drama for practice, thus removing the emotional impact from your sensitive child.

ACTIVITY #4

Everybody Sees Things Differently

Purpose: To teach your child tolerance, flexibility, and to broaden his/her perspective regarding the behaviors and feedback of others.

Rationale: The early part of every person's life is spent gathering information on how things work—objects, relationships, systems, etc. This information usually comes from a small number of people with whom the child comes into contact at home, school, church, or synagogue. Very young children take whatever they are told or shown at face value as "truth." Without more experience, your child will be unable to determine whether what s/he has been told is true or not. S/he can, however, protect him/herself against incorrect or harmful information by learning that everybody sees things differently.

Knowing that people can interpret the same events differently can save children unnecessary hurt. One six-year-old boy who had been taught this lesson, heard from his friend (a year older) that he believed his parents were pretending to be Santa Claus. To the friend, Santa was not real. When the younger boy's parent, with concern, asked him what he thought about that, he replied: "That may be so for my friend; but it definitely is not so in our family. In our family, Santa is real." The pain of learning information this boy was not ready to hear was avoided.

Tools: For very young children, one unfamiliar object whose function is unknown. For nine- to eleven-year-olds, a list of questions, one to three unfamiliar objects, and a hand-held audio tape recorder with microphone and inexpensive tape. For twelve- to fourteen-year-olds, three to five unfamiliar objects, an audio tape recorder, a video recorder, or a stenographer's notebook. To make this activity more fun, a "reporter's hat," microphone (with radio or TV call letters taped on), or "press pass" can be created to add authenticity to the investigation.

AGES 5–8 Find an object that is unfamiliar to most people (such as a ricer from the kitchen, a part from a broken tool or appliance, a specialized sewing or knitting tool, etc.). Invite your child to show this object to several people and ask each person to tell him/her what s/he thinks it is. Instruct your child to listen carefully, then say "thank you" and go to another person, each time asking only "Will you tell me what this is?" To keep things straight with very young children, accompany them and make notes on what each person says.

When four or five answers have been obtained, sit down with your child and discuss what s/he heard. With the ricer, for example, responses might be: "This is for making spaghetti. You put the dough in and squeeze it through the holes;" "This is something you use with play dough to create hair for Christmas tree angels;" "You mash potatoes and pumpkin in this;" "It's to help you squeeze out your washcloth really hard so it can dry faster;" or, "I don't know what this is!"

Together keep count of how many different answers your child got for the same object. Talk together about the fact that everybody sees things differently. Make note of the fact that people can express conviction about their own answer, even though not everybody would agree. Discuss why this might be. After this discussion, ask your child how s/he can tell if something is really true or not. Emphasize that just because someone says something strongly, or really believes what s/he says, does not make it true for the listener.

Now say to your child "I am going to tell you some things about you. Tell me what you think." Give three statements which are true and positive, such as "You listen very carefully." Then intersperse true, positive statements with silly, untrue statements. Encourage your child to respond with "That may be the way you think, but I think differently." Or, "You may think that is real, but I don't!"

One day, your child will feel hurt by what someone else has said. Draw upon this preventive activity and your practice together, saying "Tell me what you think about what that person said." Encourage your child to respond as s/he has in the past saying: "That may be what that person thinks, but it is not the way I think!" If your child disagrees with what was said, encourage him/her to say these words out loud: "Any thought that isn't mine, go right back!" When finished, ask your child to tell you how s/he feels. Most children will feel better, having released the hurt and taken back personal power.

–11 The activity is the same. However, your child will enjoy the drama of playing the part of an investigative newspaper, magazine, or television reporter finding out how people see the world in which they live. With notebook or tape recorder in hand, encourage your child to discover how many different ways a single object or idea can be viewed. Your child can write an article for a newspaper or magazine, or create a radio report which then can be read or played for you and/or the entire family. Your family can discuss the phenomenon of perspective, emphasizing how one person's truth can be entirely different from another person's truth. In your discussion, bring the conversation back to the fact that how others see us is "their truth," and not necessarily ours. Talk together about what that means when somebody tells your child something that feels hurtful. This activity will prepare him/her for easy, quick release of hurtful comments with which s/he does not agree.

2–14 The activity is the same. Children of this age, usually more aware and responsible, can utilize video reporting, if your family has a video camera or camcorder. Follow-up discussions can include an exploration of all the different ways one negative comment could be heard by a recipient. Those who are interested may also want to talk about how each person's belief system influences which interpretation s/he chooses (all people are drawn to find corroboration of internally-held beliefs).

ACTIVITY #5

Feeling the Hurt

Purpose: To legitimize and provide a time for attending to hurt feelings, and allowing time for the hurt to be expressed and pass through. Also, to create acceptance of feeling hurt within our society.

Rationale: Because "hurt" is frowned upon in our culture, most people do not learn that it is all right to take time to feel hurt feelings, to talk about them, and to provide an opportunity for the release of hurt feelings. This activity is a simple one, which provides an opportunity for expressing these behaviors.

Tools: Hurt feelings, time, and a safe, quiet place.

AGES 5–8 When you know that your child experienced a hurtful incident, or notice that your child looks sad or hurt, inquire "Are you feeling hurt inside?" If your child nods or says "yes," ask if s/he would like to be held by you. With agreement, gather your child up on your lap (or next to you where you are sitting, for a larger child), and ask him/her to tell you what has happened. If your child has no words, offer "It is okay to feel sad when you are hurt. It's okay to cry, too." If these statements trigger tears or words, even deep thought with tears welling up in your child's eyes, stay with him/her as the feelings pass. Do and say as little as possible, so your child's process is not interrupted.

When your child's tears appear to be at an end, and/or s/he shifts attention, encourage him/her to continue concentrating on the hurt feelings. Perhaps now your child will be ready to talk about the hurt, crying more as s/he does so.

Getting your child to concentrate on the hurt, directing him/her to identify where it affected his/her body, and then looking at the situation in a new way will be enough to release the pain. Afterward, if your child wants to, you can talk together about the way hurt affects us, how to let it go, and about the importance of taking time to heal and love yourself in order to recover. Talk, too, about how important it is that each of us not allow someone else to hurt us when we can tell that they are behaving in a hurtful manner. Recognize together that keeping oneself safe from hurt is one's own responsibility, both by choosing how to react to the behaviors of others, and by making certain not to let others control or hurt us deliberately.

9–11 The activity is the same. Protecting your child from exposure or criticism from others while s/he is experiencing the pain of hurt is a vital part of your job as parent. Emphasize the legitimacy of hurt feelings, as well as the internal strength it takes to express hurt.

12–14 The activity is the same. By this age, boys in particular may have already received the message that feeling and expressing hurt is less than a manly thing to do. A gentle message which states that all people feel hurt, that it takes strength to acknowledge, allow, and feel all emotions, and that feeling hurt in the privacy of one's own home is acceptable behavior, will help any young teens who have already learned that feeling hurt puts them at a disadvantage in our world. Once your young teen accepts and processes his/her hurt, internal empowerment and immunity to hurt feelings will, in fact, grow.

ACTIVITY #6

Melting the Wall of Hurt

Purpose: To symbolically create a wall of hurt feelings and then letting it melt to release the hurt and reveal our heart.

Rationale: Emotional hurt, experienced repeatedly over time, causes a child to build a protective "wall" around him/herself designed to keep him/her safe from additional hurts. Such a wall does shield your child from hurt. It also shields him/her from sharing feelings, intimacy, and getting close to others. This activity works at the subconscious level to build up and melt down the protective wall, by illustrating symbolically that your child can "melt down" emotional walls, too. Putting a heart in the very middle shows the subconscious the "prize" for melting down protective walls.

Tools: Ice cube tray, water, paper, pen or pencil, a cookie sheet or moderately deep dish. For the heart "prize," use a small paper heart, a plastic heart, a stone, a gemstone, or a candy heart.

AGES 5–8 When your child is experiencing hurt, ask him/her to talk with you about it. Ask permission to write down each of your child's hurtful experiences. Offer empathy, by saying things like "That can really hurt your feelings." Comfort your child with a hug or holding if tears are shed. When all the hurt feelings are expressed, suggest that your child do the activity.

Together draw or write the hurt feeling(s) on small pieces of paper, and fold until tiny. Create a paper heart (no larger than a dime) and color it red. Fill an ice cube tray with water and drop the tiny pieces of folded paper and the heart into separate compartments. Place the tray in your freezer for several hours until frozen. When frozen, each "hurt" will be locked inside a cube of ice. Continue the activity when the ice has hardened.

Turn the ice cubes out onto a counter or cookie sheet. Working quickly, moisten the bottom and sides of each cube, laying them “brick style” in order to create a wall. Place the cube with the heart inside on the bottom row in the middle of the “wall.” Place the other cubes randomly in the wall. Return your wall to the freezer for fifteen minutes until firm.

While the wall resets, talk with your child about hurt and how people tend to hold onto it. Discuss how holding onto hurt makes it last longer, even after your child grows up. Talk about the “wall” people build around themselves so hurt doesn’t get in and how that wall keeps them from feeling close to other people. Consider together whether or not your child wants a hurtful statement or action to keep on hurting for a long time, or whether s/he would like to release it. When you remove the wall from the freezer, tell your child that s/he can let any “wall of hurt” inside him/her melt the way this wall will melt.

Allow your child’s “wall”to melt in the sink or a dish deep enough to hold the melted ice. As your child waits for the ice to melt, s/he can create a drawing showing hurts being released, a song that says “good-bye” to hurts, or s/he can drum or dance to chase the hurt out.

Affirm together as the ice wall melts “I let any and all walls inside me melt away. I do not need a wall to protect me. I protect myself by feeling strong and good about myself.” As one of the pieces of paper listing a hurt is set free, affirm: “I release all hurts.” Making up rhymes is fun, too. “Hurt feelings melt away, making tomorrow a happier day.” As the last brick in the wall melts away, releasing the lovely red heart, you and your child can affirm: “The wall of hurt is melting and puddling; what’s left is my heart, ready for cuddling!” Allow your child to wear, display, or share his/her heart if s/he wishes.

9–11 The activity is the same. Children in this age group enjoy including family members or a friendship group.

12–14 The activity is the same. Your child may wish to include every hurt s/he can remember and create a very large wall.

ACTIVITY #7

You Hurt My Feelings

Purpose: To give your child practice and an opportunity to express hurts (real or imagined) that s/he has experienced. To provide your child with the experience of having you listen closely to his/her hurt feelings, giving time for their airing, and validating his/her experience.

Rationale: Because our culture devalues the emotion "hurt," and because additional hurt occurs when one's real hurts are not acknowledged or validated, this simple activity is healing. Taking your child's hurt feelings seriously helps heal the negative effects of hurt, shredded self-esteem and self-confidence, and annihilated feelings of love (for oneself and others). Also, learning to say what is wanted moves children out of hurt, into power.

Tools: Writing implement and paper.

AGES 5–8 On a day when your child reports feeling hurt by your actions or statements, invite him/her to sit down with you to share every hurt s/he can remember. Ask your child to share up to ten things which you have said, done, or not done which resulted in your child feeling hurt. As your child enumerates these hurts, practice "active listening." Do not interrupt, direct your attention to your child, and without defending, acknowledge each hurt by repeating your child's complaint, as in "You felt hurt when I waited in the car and didn't come in to the birthday party to get you." Jot down one or two words for each stated hurt, in order to remember what your child reports. If your child cries while sharing his/her pain, allow time for the tears. Listen carefully to your own feelings. Hearing your child's deepest hurts will evoke a feeling of empathy inside of you. Hurt used to manipulate will leave you feeling flat and non-responsive.

Next, based on your own emotional reactions and your child's conviction, together pick the three deepest hurts. These may still be painful even after your child has shared them with you. Tell your child about the words "if only," which have been described as "the two saddest words in any language." Those two words are sad because they cause us to look backward. When we are backward-focused, we cannot move or change. The only way we can unfreeze ourselves is to change the words "if only" into the words "next time."

Ask your child to tell you the three worst hurts in "if only" form. For example, "Dad [Mom], if only you had come inside to get me at the party, then I could have shown you the toy I want for my birthday!" Now you can say "I apologize for my part in you feeling hurt. What would you like me to do next time?" Use your active listening skills again to reflect your child's request. If you intend to fill the request, say so now. End your activity by thanking your child for telling you what you can do next time, since you both know a person cannot change the past, but has power in the present.

–11 The activity is the same. Using the "If only..., next time" expression can be made into a family game, used whenever members of the family are frustrated with one another's behavior. "Oh, you don't like what I did. If only I hadn't done that thing which upset you! What would you like me to do next time?" When you end the game by announcing your intention to do what is requested next time, healing and increased love and trust are the results.

–14 The activity is the same. The "If only..., next time" game for a child this age is best played with some separation. For example, when watching a television program together, you can comment out loud when one of the characters dislikes the behavior of another. For example, "I see you don't like his behavior, Ann! What do you want him to do next time?!"

ACTIVITY #8

Mrs. Murgatroyd's™* Mural

Purpose: To heal the negative effects of hurt, which takes time, and which needs to be done on both a verbal and a non-verbal level.

Rationale: Hurt, like no other emotion, takes time to heal. A mural devoted to the release and healing of hurt enables your child to continue his/her healing process as long as necessary to effect real healing.

Tools: A long piece of butcher or shelving paper which can be hung on a wall (such as a garage wall, which will not be hurt by tempera paints splashing—otherwise put plastic under the paper). A collection of pots of paint of different colors, with covers. (Plastic food "tubs" with replaceable lids are wonderful for this activity.) Paint brushes and smocks.

AGES 5–8 This activity needs very little direction from you. After determining that your child is feeling hurt, you can talk briefly with him/her about the fact that even though hurt feelings are released, later there can be more which need to come out, and more still. Because the feelings of hurt keep "seeping" out, encourage your child to take as long as s/he needs to complete this art project. Comfort your child by stating that these art supplies will be available for as long as s/he needs the project to continue. Encourage him/her to paint out feelings of hurt on the paper, providing new paper if the piece given gets filled and your child is not yet finished. Be patient. Your child may return to paint on this project after a hiatus of several days or even weeks. If at all possible, leave the mural paper and paints out and available for use for as long as three months.

*Mrs. Murgatroyd™ is a character in Enchanté's series of picture books on emotions. *William's Gift* is Enchanté's companion picture book to *Exploring Hurt With Your Child.*

9–11 The activity is the same. Encourage older children to let you know when they feel finished. Children this age can enjoy this project with friends.

12–14 The activity is the same. Young teens may wish to keep this project private and not display it for all to see. Encourage your child to let you know when s/he feels finished.

ACTIVITY #9

I Am Lovable Just the Way I Am

Purpose: To heal the effects of hurt by restoring self-love and asking for (and receiving) love from others.

Rationale: Love for others flows easily from the love felt for oneself. Self-love is necessary for making any personal change. Emotional hurt destroys love. This activity helps to restore self-love while simultaneously getting feedback, support, and love from others.

Tools: Pencil and paper for recording.

AGES 5–8 Invite your child to play a game that helps the players feel good about themselves. Form a group of two or more. You go first. Ask the "group" to wait while you move a few feet away to think. While gone, think of three things you believe are special and/or lovable about you. Return to the "group," and say "I am going to tell you three things which are special about me that I love about myself. If you agree, tell me so and if you can, give examples. Will you do it?"

Tell the first thing: "I am good at playing games." Ask your child (group) for his/her response. Get others to give examples of when you have excelled at playing games. Look squarely into the eyes of your audience members. Accept their responses with the understanding that their intentions are to give you a compliment (even if you don't totally agree with what is said), and receive them with a smile. When all the responses for that example are complete, say "thank you" and go on to the other two examples. At the end of your turn, encourage your audience to give you a round of applause.

Now, change places with your child. S/he goes off to think of three things which are lovable about him/her, while you become the audience. Follow the same procedure, ending with a big round of applause for your child! You and your child (group) may enjoy going around again, with three more lovable qualities shared by each person.

–11 This activity is the same. Your child may become very silly, having a difficult time accepting positive energy and love. If so, challenge your child to listen to feedback for two minutes without laughing or smiling, responding only with a "thank you." Take care, also, that the members of the group are giving feedback which is very specific: instead of "you're a good friend," say "I like the way you support me by cheering loudly when I have a soccer game."

2–14 The activity is the same. A variation that might be easier for a young teen would be for him/her to listen to the affirmations without facing the audience. Have him/her write the three things down on separate pieces of paper and place them in the center of the group. S/he then turns around, with his/her back facing the group. The people in the group make their positive comments out loud, as though your child is not there, telling each other their validation of the claims. Your child keeps busy taking written notes of what is said, leaving him/her with a list of positive things said about him/her in support of his/her lovable qualities. Allow applause when all comments have been made and your child turns to rejoin the group. The list can be displayed publicly or viewed in private to reinforce the positive messages.

ACTIVITY #10

In My World, My Policy Is...

Purpose: To heal the negative effects of hurt, particularly shredded self-confidence and self-esteem, powerlessness, and the intrusion of personal boundaries.

Rationale: Whenever a "problem" arises in your child's life, s/he has a choice: either s/he can attempt to "fix the problem," or take steps to "become the person s/he would be without the 'problem'." The same choice exists when emotional hurt has occurred. "Fixing" focuses your child backward and keeps him/her stuck. "Becoming" focuses your child forward, freeing him/her for growth. Once the tears and pain of the hurt have been released, your child heals fastest by focusing on what s/he wants to "become."

Since most hurtful experiences between people result from manipulative behavior, using a tool that protects against and deflects manipulation will allow your child to heal that damage. Creating a personal policy which your child can implement is such a tool. When your child can respond to a hurtful remark with "I do not allow other people to say mean things about me; instead, I walk away when the first statement is made," s/he will strengthen personal boundaries, mend self-esteem, build self-confidence, create self-love (vital for making any personal change), and not experience further hurt.

Tools: A cape (see *Exploring Fear With Your Child*, Activity #4), crown, or other prop which your child can use to feel empowered. A list of experiences that have been hurtful to your child.

Ages 5–8 On a day when your child's confidence is already high, ask him/her if s/he would like to join you in an activity that will establish good feelings that s/he can recall in the event that his/her feelings are hurt in the future. Explain the activity this way: "People don't always mean to hurt others. When you are not feeling strong inside, other children can somehow tell, and that's when you get hurt the most. When you are feeling strong, other people usually do not do so much that is deliberately hurtful. If you have to take a moment to decide each time what to do when another person is hurtful, you may seem weak. But if you have what we call a 'policy,' you are stronger. A 'policy' is something you do every time a particular thing happens. My policy with you is 'Every time you are dressed for bed, have washed your face and brushed your teeth and hair, I read you a story.' Would you like to make some policies about what to do when you get hurt in the future so you can be strong on those days?"

With your child's agreement, have him/her help you make a list of all the things s/he can think of that have felt hurtful in the past. Explain that the two of you will now work together to create policies to neutralize that hurt.

Placing the "power prop" on your child's head or shoulders, have him/her stand up high (atop a stool, a set of stairs, or on a large chair or sofa. Read aloud one of his/her hurtful experiences, and ask: "If you were the king or queen of your own land, what policy would you make to be sure you never were hurt by this again?" This question gets your child to think beyond "limitation," looking for what can be done if s/he had no limits. Help your child find a strong policy.

Once the policy is selected, have your child assume the pose of a monarch, ready to make a proclamation. Making a sweeping gesture with his/her arm or cape, have him/her state: "From this moment forward, whenever anyone even tries to call me a name, I will turn my back and walk away." Or, "From this moment forward, I will give help to other people whenever they are able to ask for it directly." One by one, go down the "hurt list" and create policies together, until the list is finished. Write the "policy list" down next to the "hurt list." (You and your child may wish for you as the adult to take a turn at policy-making, too!) When the proclamations are finished, you and your child can create a chart or pictures that remind him/her of the new policies. This chart can be referred to in the future when hurt is experienced.

Ages 9–11 The activity is the same. Children of this age may enjoy making a stage production out of the activity, with more than one child creating policies and making proclamations. If several children experience a similar hurt, they can make a group proclamation, finding strength in togetherness. Be certain to guide this activity so that your child is not setting him/herself up to deliberately hurt someone else, or to act in ways that will damage his/her own self-esteem. For the next several days, you and your child can talk about this activity, sharing the success of getting out of situations where you feel "one-down" by creating a personal policy and announcing it to others in the family. You may be surprised how much interpersonal conflict will decrease following the completion of this activity.

Ages 12–14 Your young teen may feel "too old" for this "king of the mountain" activity. S/he may prefer to make a list of hurts, create policies, and announce them out loud. A few minutes spent with his/her eyes closed will allow him/her time to imagine what following this policy will feel like, now that s/he has given him/herself permission to have this feeling. Writing down personal policies and saying them aloud gives them more strength in your young teen's mind. It might feel safer and avoid possible embarassment for your young teen to use the protagonists of news stories, television dramas, or life situations of friends to consider what policies would protect that person from hurt rather than considering his/her own.

Hurt plays a bigger role in most people's lives than they realize. Discouraged from acknowledging and sharing real hurt feelings, people wrongly use hurt to control and manipulate others. Manipulation destroys love and creates more hurt. Emotional hurt shreds both self-esteem and self-confidence, and holding onto feelings of hurt becomes a heavy burden. Fortunately, it is not a burden that your child needs to carry throughout life.

The emotional work that this booklet, and this series, assists you to do (in fun!) can create a relationship of trust and deep joy between you and your child which most people seldom experience. When parents ***a)*** take care to avoid hurting children emotionally; ***b)*** teach children to recognize manipulation attempts and refuse to allow hurt to be used manipulatively toward them; and ***c)*** help children to feel, process, release, and recover from hurt feelings, then love, improved self-image, and self-confidence are restored. In working on hurt with your child, perhaps you have strengthened your own ability to diffuse, process, and heal from emotionally hurtful situations in your life as well.

The bonds of love and respect between you and your child grow whenever you work in partnership to develop your abilities for navigating the sometimes tricky "emotional waters" of life.

About the Author

Ilene L. Dillon, M.S.W., L.C.S.W., and M.F.C.C., is the originator of "Conscious Parenting," a practical method which redefines the job of parenting and the role of children so that children are led to conscious, self-directed choice. In this new partnership model, the child teaches the parent, too, providing permission for everyone to grow and change.

Mother of two, Ilene has experienced parenting as both a married and a single parent. She is the author of a series of self-help booklets, "The Bounce Back Series," and maintains a private psychotherapy practice in Fairfax, California. She is a professional speaker, and has lectured in both the United States and Australia. She is also a member of the National Speakers Association.

A division of the international children's media company, Enchanté, Ltd., Enchanté Publishing was formed in 1991. A unique publishing house, the company has assembled an advisory board comprised of leading educators, physicians, therapists, and business executives who provide a multicultural and multidisciplinary approach to making irresistible educational materials for children.

Enchanté books and other products are on the leading edge of a new trend toward Emotional Literacy™—the ability to recognize, understand, and appropriately express our emotions. Enchanté has developed three series of companion titles including picture books, activity books, and parents' guides that can be used together to build Emotional Literacy™.

The picture books take children to the enchanted world of Mrs. Murgatroyd™ and her magical paints. Developed by Liz Farrington, a respected art and play therapist who has worked with children for more than 25 years, these stories were drawn from true accounts. The children's activity books are designed to help children identify, explore, and express their emotions through fun, Inner-Active activities. The parents' guides, written by Ilene Dillon, a licensed clinical social worker, were developed to help parents recognize and understand what their child is experiencing, and provide fun, creative activities to assist their child in expressing his/her feelings in a constructive way.

Enchanté Publishing
1250 Sixth Street, Suite 403
Santa Monica, CA 90401

ORDERED BY:

Name ______________________________

Address ______________________________

City/State/Zip code ______________________________

Phone ______________________________

SHIP TO: (if different from address above)

Name ______________________________

Address ______________________________

City/State/Zip code ______________________________

Phone ______________________________

All prices subject to change without notice

Standard discount rates apply

____
Ship Date:

____
Purchase Order Number:

____
Signature:

Do Not Backorder: ❑

FOR INFORMATION CALL:

(800) 473-2363 or **(415) 617-9400**

FAX # (415) 473-1078

Complete order information on reverse side

ORDER QTY.	ISBN	DESCRIPTION	SUG. RETAIL	DISC.	TOTAL COST
	1-56844-040-5	Knight-time for Brigitte™ (HC/All ages) (AVAILABLE IN DECEMBER, 1994)	$12.95		
		EMOTION SERIES			
	1-56844-000-6	And Peter Said Goodbye (HC/Ages 5 & up)	$14.95		
	1-56844-050-2	Exploring Grief—Activity Book (Ages 5–9)	$ 3.95		
	1-56844-064-2	Exploring Grief With Your Child—Parents' Guide	$ 4.95		
	1-56844-003-0	Nightmares in the Mist (HC/Ages 5 & up)	$14.95		
	1-56844-053-7	Exploring Fear—Activity Book (Ages 5–9)	$ 3.95		
	1-56844-068-5	Exploring Fear With Your Child—Parents' Guide	$ 4.95		
	1-56844-001-4	Painting the Fire (HC/Ages 5 & up)	$14.95		
	1-56844-051-0	Exploring Anger—Activity Book (Ages 5–9)	$ 3.95		
	1-56844-065-0	Exploring Anger With Your Child—Parents' Guide	$ 4.95		
	1-56844-004-9	The Rainbow Fields (HC/Ages 5 & up)	$14.95		
	1-56844-054-5	Exploring Loneliness—Activity Book (Ages 5–9)	$ 3.95		
	1-56844-067-7	Exploring Loneliness With Your Child—Parents' Guide	$ 4.95		
	1-56844-005-7	Red Poppies for a Little Bird (HC/Ages 5 & up)	$14.95		
	1-56844-055-3	Exploring Guilt—Activity Book (Ages 5–9)	$ 3.95		
	1-56844-069-3	Exploring Guilt With Your Child—Parents' Guide	$ 4.95		
	1-56844-002-2	Tanya and the Green-Eyed Monster (HC/Ages 5 & up)	$14.95		
	1-56844-052-9	Exploring Jealousy—Activity Book (Ages 5–9)	$ 3.95		
	1-56844-066-9	Exploring Jealousy With Your Child—Parents' Guide	$ 4.95		
	1-56844-007-3	William's Gift (HC/Ages 5 & up)	$14.95		
	1-56844-057-X	Exploring Hurt—Activity Book (Ages 5–9)	$ 3.95		
	1-56844-070-7	Exploring Hurt With Your Child—Parents' Guide	$ 4.95		
		COLOR SERIES (AVAILABLE IN EARLY 1995)			
	1-56844-025-1	The Magic of Red (HC/Ages 3–8)	$ 6.95		
	1-56844-026-X	The Magic of Orange (HC/Ages 3–8)	$ 6.95		
	1-56844-027-8	The Magic of Yellow (HC/Ages 3–8)	$ 6.95		
	1-56844-028-6	The Magic of Green (HC/Ages 3–8)	$ 6.95		
	1-56844-029-4	The Magic of Blue (HC/Ages 3–8)	$ 6.95		
	1-56844-031-6	The Magic of Purple (HC/Ages 3–8)	$ 6.95		
	Item Total				

SUBTOTAL	$_____
Postage (domestic within U.S.) 7.5% of subtotal	$_____
Postage (overseas) 10% of subtotal	$_____
Handling Charge (on all orders within U.S.)	$ 3.00
Handling Charge (overseas, add $3.00)	$_____
Tax (California residents add 8.25%)	$_____
GRAND TOTAL	$_____

Please make checks payable to:
ENCHANTÉ LTD.
Send to :
Enchanté Publishing
1250 Sixth St. #403
Santa Monica, CA 90401
Checks must accompany order

HC = Hardcover